# OUR  WILDERNESS

# OUR WILDERNESS

## HOW THE PEOPLE OF NEW YORK
### FOUND, CHANGED AND PRESERVED
### THE ADIRONDACKS

BY

## MICHAEL STEINBERG

ADIRONDACK MOUNTAIN CLUB, INC.
LAKE GEORGE, NEW YORK • 1992

Published by the Adirondack Mountain Club, Inc.
R.R. 3, Box 3055, Lake George, New York 12845

**Library of Congress Cataloging-in-Publication Data**

Steinberg, Michael.
    Our wilderness : how the people of New York found, changed, and
    preserved the Adirondacks / by Michael Steinberg.
        p.    cm.
    Includes index.
    Summary: Describes how the Adirondack Park of New York State was
created in 1892 to preserve over a million acres of land and keep it
"forever wild."
    ISBN 0-935272-56-9 : $18.95
    1. Adirondack Park (N.Y.)--History--Juvenile literature.
2. Conservation of natural resources--New York (State)--Adirondack
Park--History--Juvenile literature.   [1. Adirondack Park (N.Y.)-
-History. 2. Conservation of natural resources--New York (State)-
-Adirondack Park--History.]   I. Adirondack Mountain Club.
II. Title.                                                      91-16550
F127.A2S64 1992                                                 CIP
974.7'5--dc20                                                   AC

Edited by Neal S. Burdick
Typography and design by Jim Benvenuto
Maps by Elayne Sears
Cover photograph by Michael Steinberg
Printed and bound in the United States of America

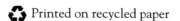 Printed on recycled paper

Celebrating the Adirondack Park Centennial

1892

1992

A park of people and natural wonder

## Acknowledgments

Even as small a book as this is the work of many hands. My son Paul's interest in the Adirondacks inspired my writing, and many others added their encouragement or criticism along the way. The enthusiasm of Read Kingsbury of ADK's publications committee and publications director Carmen Elliott has not flagged from the day I first contacted them. Jim Benvenuto, our designer, knew the format I wanted better than I knew myself.

Vickie Curry, Paul's third-grade teacher at School 23 in Rochester, New York, gave my confidence a welcome boost. Sarah Comstock of Wildwood in Old Forge made some important corrections and suggestions. Trent Aldous, Kate Barton, Paul Grant, Patrick Guarasci, Rachel McKnight, Scott Matott, Emily Moody, Jason Stromgren, May Tolly and Stacy Van Brocklin — all students at McKenney Middle School in Canton, New York — read an earlier draft of the book and sent me some thought-provoking criticism. (I hope I've spelled everyone's name correctly!) If I have erred in detail or failed to make the book useful it is my own fault.

Terry Wendt of Star Lake showed me the Benson Mine pit, told me about work at the mine, and helped me get a photograph that I hope tells some of the story.

The help I received when looking for illustrations went far beyond what I expected. The standard photo credit reads "courtesy of so-and-so." In the present case the word "courtesy" should be taken literally.

Not the least credit must go to the J. M. Kaplan Fund, whose generous support made it possible for us to produce the book Carmen, Jim and I envisioned. To all, including those whose names I have omitted in error, my deepest thanks.

# Table of Contents

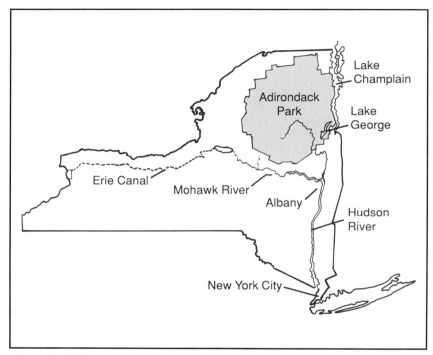

*New York State*

## One. An Introduction

WHEN MOST PEOPLE think of New York they think of New York City. It is one of the largest cities in the world; 15 million people live in and around it. It is the heart of American culture and business and one of the world's great tourist centers.

But there is much more to New York State than a city. North from New York harbor and the Statue of Liberty stretches the Hudson River. Its beautiful valley, a narrow, rocky corridor through the Appalachian highlands, was an important water route for the early fur traders. It is still the route "Upstate" for many roads and railroads.

About 140 miles north along the Hudson is Albany, once a great fur-trading center and now the state capital. From the tops of the tall government buildings in Albany you can see hills rising to the north. These are the foothills of the Adirondacks, New York's highest mountains. In half a day you can ride from the country's largest city to one of its largest parks, the Adirondack Park.

The Adirondack Park, which was created in 1892, is not like any other park in the United States. About 60 percent of it is private land, with homes, schools, stores and other businesses.

There are villages, timberlands, mines and factories where people have lived and worked for over a hundred years. But the rest of the Park — the Adirondack Forest Preserve — is owned by the people of New York, and in 1894 they chose to leave these lands "forever wild." That law is part of New York State's constitution. No single legislature can change it, even to allow one tree to be felled or one cabin built. No other land of the United States has stronger protection.

The Adirondack Park is bigger than eight of the states. It contains more than 9,000 square miles of mountains, lakes, rivers, villages, farms and forests; only Alaska has a larger park. The state wilderness areas alone contain more than half the protected wilderness east of the Mississippi.

On the state lands the beech, spruce, hemlock and pine, white and yellow birch and balsam grow and die as they have for centuries. Dead trees fall and rot, covered with moss and little orange or great white mushrooms. New trees struggle up from the forest floor, searching for light. Beavers dam streams and turn them into beaver ponds. The ponds fill in and become grassy meadows. Shrubs and trees sprout and deer and bear forage among the new growth. Then the forest closes in once more, until a new colony of beavers builds another dam.

From many mountains in the Park you can look out over endless forest — the kind of view Native Americans and the first European settlers saw. One of them is Black Bear Mountain. This little peak, near Old Forge in the western Adirondacks, shows a great deal about the Adirondacks and their history.

For the first mile the trail up Black Bear Mountain is a grassy road. It passes a little swamp, a beaver's work. Soon boulders and low cliffs rise behind the trees on the left. The trail was once a private road built for the wealthy banker J.P. Morgan. A hundred years ago he had a "great camp" on nearby Mohegan Lake — buildings for himself and his servants and his guests, a place to get away from it all. Now somebody else owns the

*Looking northeast from Black Bear Mountain. (Photo by author)*

camp, the forest is closing in and the old Uncas Road is the
Uncas Trail; but it is still easy to imagine Morgan in his six-
horse coach, driving from the railroad to his lakeside kingdom.

About three-quarters of the way up the mountain is a shelf of
rock. The view is framed by the side of the mountain and a tree.
Rolls of blue-green mountains rise one behind the other into
the distance. In the summer light they turn bluer and fainter
until you cannot tell them apart from distant clouds.

Closer at hand is a valley, yellow-green with bushes and grass
between the dark green of the hills. Through the valley No
Luck Brook makes its patient way back and forth. You are far
enough from roads that you can hear no cars. There seems nothing here that was made by a human hand.

Nothing, that is, but the view itself. The wilderness you look
into was once a wasteland. For a century lumbermen worked

over almost every inch of the Adirondacks. Almost every mountain was stripped bare. Almost every stream ran brown with mud from ruined, gullied hillsides.

In the early 1900s great fires burned through the Adirondack forests. Sparks from coal-burning locomotives started many of them. The charred tree trunks left by the fire gave Black Bear Mountain its name. The heat was so great it burned even the soil, and after eighty years the blueberry bushes and small trees are only beginning to cover the rocky summit.

But the forest is returning. Nature heals itself. We nearly destroyed the forests, but we also let them rebuild. After we discovered the mountains we conquered them, used them, and looted them. Then we drew back. We returned some of them to nature and promised never to harm those lands again. That promise was made for practical, businesslike reasons, not for love of wilderness, and we have not always kept it. But we have done better than anyone might have guessed. And nature, in its turn, has given us one of the richest and most beautiful places in the world.

## Two. Beginnings

T HE ADIRONDACK MOUNTAINS are not the highest mountains in the United States, or even in the East. The tallest peak, Mount Marcy, is just over a mile above sea level. There are dozens of other mountains, though, steep and rocky and carved into fantastic shapes or rounded and forest-covered, and hundreds of hills and ridges. Great passes split the ranges. At the bottom of Indian Pass, in the shade of Wallface Mountain, ice caves breathe out chilled air in even the hottest August.

Within the Adirondack Park are hundreds of wild rivers and streams, waterfalls beyond number, rolling hills, scrubby flood plains and thousands of lakes. The western half of the Park has more lakes than mountains. There are little ponds hidden in swampland and deep sapphire lakes dotted with islands, like Blue Mountain Lake. There are chains of interconnected lakes, favorite places to canoe and to build summer homes.

Many of the early vacationers thought of this lake country as "the Adirondacks." It was an easier country to visit than the mountains to the east. Anyone with a few dollars could hire a guide and a boat. The guide pulled the oars, and the tourist sat back and relaxed.

Near the center of the Park the mountains begin to climb higher: Blue Mountain, Wakely Mountain, and steep Snowy Mountain all rise close to 4,000 feet. Farther east is the High Peaks region, the true mountain country and what most visitors today think of as "the Adirondacks." Five ranges run southwest

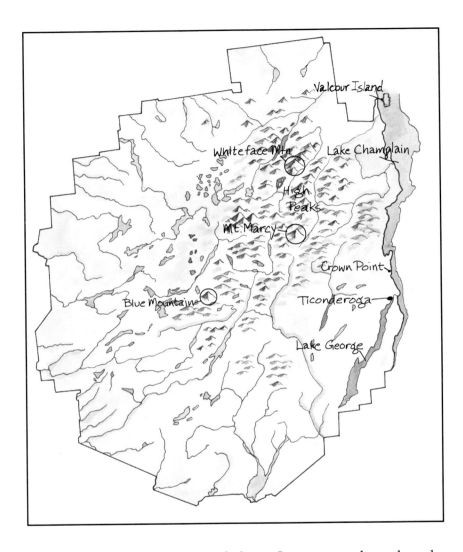

Valcour Island

Whiteface Mtn

Lake Champlain

High Peaks

Mt. Marcy

Crown Point

Blue Mountain

Ticonderoga

Lake George

to northeast. Many peaks stand alone. Streams cut through rock shelves and rush past great boulders in every direction to the Hudson, Mohawk or St. Lawrence rivers. The few lakes are hidden between rocky walls, or cower under stone cliffs.

Then, in a few short miles, the mountain country ends. Just 40 miles from the top of Mount Marcy is Lake Champlain, only 95 feet above sea level.

*For over a hundred years the low hills and many lakes of the western and central Adirondacks have been popular vacation spots. (Photo by author)*

Lake country or mountains, the Adirondacks are all built from the same stubborn, hard rock. They are a southern part of the Canadian Shield, the ancient rock that makes up most of Ontario and Quebec. Shield rock is unbelievably old — the crust of the earth, usually buried under layers of sediment.

The first Adirondacks rose more than a billion years ago. A great oval bubble of rock welled up from deep in the earth like the shell of a stone turtle. We do not know how high those first mountains were. Wind and rain and ice wore them down to almost nothing.

For a time an ocean covered the worn-down hills. Then another mountain range grew. Over hundreds of millions of years it, too, was scoured away by erosion. Time and time again glaciers poured down from Canada, wearing down peaks and scooping out valleys. When the last Ice Age ended, about 12,000 years ago, all that was left was the bare rock that had risen a billion years before. It is rising still. The Adirondacks are growing more than an inch every century.

*The time-scarred slopes of Gothics, one of the High Peaks. (Photo by author)*

It was cold and lifeless after the ice melted. The lakes were clear pools of melted water. There was little soil on the mountains. Sand and gravel had been dumped by the melting glaciers to form wide plains and winding eskers. No forests grew in the bare rock and sand.

On the bare mountainsides the sun heated the rock. The winter ice cracked boulders open. Soon patches of lichen spread over the bare stone, dissolving the rock with the acids they produce, their tiny roots searching out every new crack. As they grew and died they made new soil.

The first plants to sprout in the rocky soil were arctic plants, tiny flowering shrubs that now are found only on the tops of the highest Adirondack peaks. Their seeds either blew in on the winds or were carried by birds.

Mosses, then grasses and then small bushes took over. Their roots trapped every bit of the precious soil. As they died and rotted they became part of the soil themselves. Year after year the new soil built up, and the plants grew larger and larger. Ten thousand years after the glaciers left, a new forest stood where there had once been bare rock and sand.

The climate grew warmer after the glaciers left, and the arctic plants now lived only on the windy mountaintops. Cold-loving animals like the moose and the snowshoe hare retreated to the mountainsides. The Adirondacks became a special island of life on a special island of rock, surrounded by an ocean of lowland forest. To this day poison ivy grows in just a few spots in the Park, and poisonous snakes live only on its eastern edge.

As the ice melted, Native Americans began to explore the mountains; but they found them too rough, too wild and cold. There was little soil rich enough for their corn to grow. They sent hunting parties to the mountains in summer to bring back moose, deer and bear, but they built their villages in the lowlands along the Mohawk and St. Lawrence rivers, the shores

*The "arctic-alpine" zone on the highest of the High Peaks preserves the climate and the plants that followed the last ice age. Climbing a mountain like Haystack, third-highest in the Adirondacks, is like walking 10,000 years into the past. (Photo by author)*

of Lake Ontario to the west and the Finger Lakes to the south-west. (Today the Adirondacks are full of Indian names, but many of them were invented for tourists. There is no real evidence, for example, that Indian Pass was part of an Indian path. Even Tahawus, the "Indian name" for Mount Marcy, was the invention of a writer in the 1830s. It is actually a word in Seneca, the language of an Indian nation 200 miles away in western New York.)

The nations south of the Adirondacks were Iroquois. The mountains formed a barrier between them and their enemies,

[ 9 ]

the Huron nations to the north. Warriors passed through from time to time, but most war parties took an easier trail. One arm of Y-shaped Lake George pushes close to Lake Champlain, so the two long lakes make a water route, with some interruptions, from the Hudson Valley all the way to the St. Lawrence.

The Iroquois and Huron might have warred on these lakes forever, but the European settlers made the Indian wars part of a bigger, more deadly struggle. In 1609 Samuel de Champlain, a Frenchman on an exploring trip with his Huron allies, encountered a band of Iroquois near Lake Champlain. The French fired on the Iroquois. Most books say that this shot started a feud that lasted until the French were driven out of Canada in 1763.

If that gun had never been fired, though, the feud might well have started some other way. The English and the French were enemies. The water route along the lakes was an important link in the fur trade, and in those days furs, especially beaver pelts, were the most valuable products of the American forests. Both sides wanted to control that wealth.

Through the 1700s France and England fought time and time again. It was the first real world war. There was fighting at sea and in Europe, America and India. The English recruited the Iroquois as allies and the French recruited the Huron.

The European generals saw that they could control this important water route if they held the land between Lake George and Lake Champlain. They built great forts there. In 1731 the French built Fort St. Frederic on Crown Point, and in 1755 they began to build Fort Carillon — the fort that we know today by the name the English gave it, Ticonderoga. In 1757 the French general Montcalm captured Fort William Henry, the English fort on Lake George.

Only a year later, on their third try in three years, the English took all the forts and forced the French off the lakes. Montcalm himself was killed the next year at the great battle of Quebec, on the Plains of Abraham. When the war ended, in 1763, the

*The ruins of Crown Point still stand sentry above Lake Champlain. (Photo courtesy New York State Office of Parks and Recreation)*

English ruled all of eastern North America.

They did not keep it for long. In May of 1775, at the dawn of the American Revolution, Ethan Allen and his "Green Mountain Boys" came across Lake Champlain from Vermont. In the middle of the night they demanded the surrender of Ticonderoga "in the name of the Great Jehovah and the Continental Congress." The startled commander agreed.

The first American navy fought on Lake Champlain. To meet an English army invading from Canada, Benedict Arnold had hurriedly built a fleet. On October 11, 1776, he and his men held off the English for seven hours near Valcour Island and escaped through the enemy lines as the day ended. Arnold's own flagship went down. It looked as if the Americans had lost, but they had delayed the English so long that the invasion was called off.

The next year the English retook the lakes and marched

*An English officer painted this picture of the Battle of Valcour Island. (Windsor Castle, Royal Library. © 1991 Her Majesty Queen Elizabeth II)*

south to Saratoga. The American colonists were better armed and better organized by then. Their victory was so complete that the cause of independence was saved.

After the Battle of Saratoga the Adirondacks begin to slip out of history again. During the War of 1812 another British invasion was held off at a bloody naval battle on Lake Champlain. When peace came, though, the forts were left to fall into ruins.

But the Europeans had begun to make their mark in the mountains. Through all the wars two things had remained constant. Europe needed pine trees and it wanted beaver.

Tall white pines grew a hundred feet high on the shores of Lake George and Lake Champlain. Even in the 1600s they were being felled to make masts for sailing ships.

Even more precious than pine trees were beaver pelts. The best hats were made from beaver, and in Europe the beaver had been trapped almost to extinction. From the early 1600s Indians and Europeans roamed the forests trapping. They brought their beaver skins to the great centers of the fur trade: Montreal, Boston and Albany. By the 1800s there were almost no beaver left in the mountains. Dark forest closed in where beaver ponds had once drowned trees and opened up clearings. The first great change in the Adirondacks had happened almost invisibly.

While armies and navies struggled on the Adirondacks' eastern edge, and while unknown trappers wandered the forests, the rest of the world paid no attention to the region. It was said to be a swampy and dismal place. Nobody lived there, and nothing of interest lay there. If the trappers knew differently they did not say. As late as 1810 geography books claimed that no mountain in the region rose higher than 1300 feet above sea level. The Adirondacks remained a mystery.

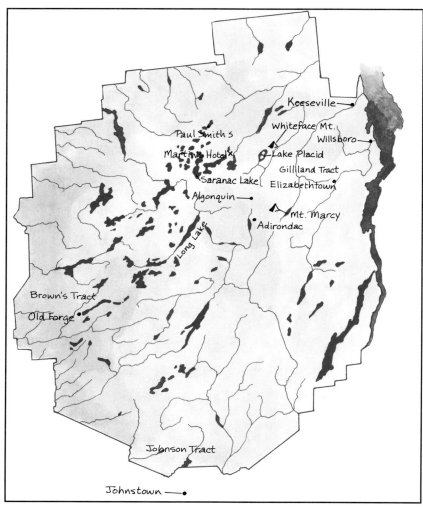

*The Adirondacks in the early 1800s.*

## Three. The Treasure Seekers

S OME PEOPLE HAD TRIED to settle the mountains.
In the middle of the 1700s Sir William Johnson built a
trading center he called Johnstown and a great mansion for his
family. A close friend of the Iroquois, he ruled over much of the
southern Adirondacks.

Later, on the Boquet River near Lake Champlain, William
Gilliland carved out farms and towns and lured settlers to what
he himself called "a howling wilderness." He was full of energy
and ideas. He had chosen one of the most fertile sites in all the
mountains, and for a few years his colony grew. But the Revolu-
tionary War passed right through his land. In 1776, as Benedict
Arnold's troops retreated from a failed attempt to conquer
Canada, they took refuge on Gilliland's estate. Gilliland treated
them warmly, at his own expense. But Arnold accused him of
cheating the soldiers and Gilliland was thrown into prison.

He was later released, but his troubles were just starting. The
British, marching toward Saratoga the next year, took what was
left of Gilliland's crops and stock. The state and national governments refused to pay him for his services and his losses. His

property and money gone, Gilliland found work with surveyors near his old home. Sometimes he rode his old estate, still thinking he owned it. One winter day he wandered alone into the woods. Days later his body was found, frozen. All that was left of Gilliland's colony were two names: Willsboro, which he named after himself, and Elizabethtown, named after his wife.

Most American pioneers looked to the west. Almost all of the Indian nations along the Great Lakes and the Ohio Valley had been allies of the British, and an English law had promised that land to the Indians. But the new United States was not bound by the law. It gave the land to soldiers and their families or sold it cheaply to anyone else.

In this "Northwest Territory" the climate was good and the land rich. The hills were low and rolling. It was good land to plow and harvest, much better than the steep, stony hills of the Adirondacks.

The state of New York set aside part of the Adirondacks to help pay off soldiers from the Revolution. Not one soldier took up the offer of free land. They moved west instead.

So the state followed the settlers. Armies of workmen dug the Erie Canal from Albany to Buffalo. It was the best and cheapest route from the Atlantic Ocean to the Great Lakes, and new cities and farms grew up along its path. With the west growing so rapidly there was no reason to consider the cold, rugged Adirondacks.

There were a few exceptions. Since nobody wanted the land in the mountains it could be bought for almost nothing. In 1791 the state sold four and a half million acres to Alexander Macomb. He paid 16 cents an acre. Even though 16 cents in 1791 would be worth several dollars in today's money, the sale was still a tremendous bargain.

Part of the Macomb Purchase was bought seven years later by John Brown. (The abolitionist John Brown lived and is buried near Lake Placid; this John Brown came from the wealthy family that gave its name to Brown University in Rhode Island.) An old and popular story says that Brown's son-in-law traded a ship's cargo for the land, like Jack in the fairy tale trading his cow for three worthless-looking beans. It is said that John Brown burst into tears at the news. The story is not true. We know now that he had wanted the land for some time.

The Brown's Tract — it is still known as that — took in some 200,000 acres in the west-central Adirondacks. John Brown surveyed townships and gave them names: Industry, Enterprise, Perseverance, Regularity, Unanimity, Frugality and Sobriety. These were the virtues he expected from his settlers.

But not even enterprise, industry, frugality and the rest were enough. John Brown pushed a road through the wilderness, but it was still a long, rough, difficult and expensive route to travel. Once his settlers arrived they faced the same problems Adirondack farmers struggle with today. Summer comes late. Winter comes early and is as cold and snowy as anything in New England, or worse. The center of Brown's Tract has recorded temperatures more than fifty degrees below zero, and in many winters more than 10 feet of snow has fallen. The stony soil is poor in nutrients, and the many hills and valleys make it hard to plow and plant.

Brown set up two settlements. At one he built a sawmill and a grist mill. A few settlers came, but none stayed long. When Brown died in 1803 the settlement seemed dead forever.

But in 1811 Brown's son-in-law, Charles Herreshoff, decided to move to the family tract. At first he, too, tried to attract farmers. Then he decided to try grazing. The hills and lakes of the area were often compared to Scotland's, and the cold climate, Herreshoff must have thought, would ensure heavy, valuable fleece. This, too, came to nothing.

In 1817 Herreshoff turned to iron mining. He knew that the Adirondacks held many small pockets of iron ore; the hills around Lake Champlain had been mined as early as the 1700s.

*Charles Herreshoff's house — the "Herreshoff Manor" — when it was being used as a hotel. (Photo courtesy the Adirondack Museum)*

Herreshoff borrowed money to start a mine, build a forge, and make the charcoal to smelt the ore. He produced a few bars of iron, too poor in quality to be worth carrying out of the mountains. In December of 1819 one of his newest iron mines flooded and caved in. Herreshoff went to inspect the damage, returned home in despair and shot himself. The settlement soon vanished.

The remains of the "old forge" became a landmark. Years later, when a village grew up on its site, it became known as Old Forge — now the biggest village in the western Adirondacks and a popular vacation spot. Of John Brown's other settlement nothing at all remains. "Middle Settlement" Lake lies in a state wilderness area.

The sad story of the Brown's Tract is not unusual. Throughout the mountains little villages or isolated farmers struggled against bad weather, poor soil, rough muddy roads and loneliness. In the valleys, where the climate was kinder and the soil better, some farmers prospered. But their prosperity was often an illusion. One harsh winter or one spring flood could destroy everything. Some towns were abandoned only a few years after they were founded, never to be rebuilt.

In the 1840s a New England minister, John Todd, came to Long Lake. Here, in the very center of the Adirondacks, about eighteen families were trying to survive, adding to their meager crops by hunting and fishing.

Todd was vacationing — he was one of the first Adirondack tourists — but he lost no chance to preach, and the Long Lakers seemed ready to listen. At his urging they set up a church. Todd returned home to raise money and collect books for his new flock. He was certain that the settlement had a great future.

Like many others at the time, Todd believed that trees kept the weather cold by keeping the ground shaded. Chop down the forests, he wrote, and the Adirondacks would become warm and fertile. A million farmers would grow wheat and graze cattle on the grassy slopes. Civilization would come to the mountains.

But it was not to be — luckily, because chopping down the trees would not have changed the Adirondack winters. The villagers of Long Lake accepted the money and books Rev. Todd sent them, but they never became the model farmers he hoped for. Long Lake survived because it was the home of the area's best hunting and fishing guides. One of them, Mitchell Sabattis, was also a powerful leader in the village's Methodist church, so Todd left a mark of sorts. But the million farmers never came.

Life was hard in the villages, but it was even harder for the families that lived alone. William Martin came to the Saranac lakes in 1849. He built a hotel, but for years there were no roads leading to Martin's, no town, and only a handful of neighbors.

Worse yet, the closest doctor lived in Keeseville, 45 miles away. In the winter of 1862, a bad winter in a country of bad

*Long Lake soon after the time of John Todd. (Photo courtesy the Adirondack Museum)*

winters, Martin's ten-year-old daughter, Laura Ann, took sick. A blizzard had shut the only road out, but Martin, terrified, was determined to fetch the doctor. With horse and sleigh, and armed with an ax and a shovel, he plowed and dug through the 12-foot snow drifts. He wore his horse out on the way to Keeseville, found the doctor, hitched a new horse to the sleigh and returned without a rest. But he was too late. Laura Ann had died fifteen minutes before he arrived.

Martin was so shaken by her death that he began studying medicine. He read whatever books he could find and asked advice from the doctors who stayed at his hotel. For years he was both a hotel-keeper and an amateur doctor, treating all his patients for free. When at last a professional doctor settled in Saranac Lake, "Doctor" Martin happily ended his medical career.

Most settlers were defeated by the hardships. There seemed to be only one exception. For thirty years the iron works of Adirondac (as it was spelled) were the center of a busy, growing town. The village sat by one of the richest ore beds known, and some of the first steel made in America came from its ore.

Archibald McIntyre, Malcolm McMartin and David Henderson had been early pioneers in the Adirondack iron industry. Their iron works near Lake Placid had been founded in 1809, but it was not until 1826 that the great discovery was made. An Indian, Lewis Elijah, showed Henderson a piece of rich iron ore and offered to show him the source for $1.50 and a wad of tobacco.

Henderson and his partners followed Elijah to a river that ran through a vast bed of iron ore. They rushed at once to the capital in Albany to file their claim and set up their company.

By 1838 there was a small town around the iron works. David Henderson managed the business, and his energy and intelligence made it a success. The town had a school and a bank. Henderson visited England to study its steel industry, and made plans to build a steel mill.

By the middle 1840s the works at Adirondac were producing twelve to fourteen tons of iron a day. The forge needed more water, so Henderson, his son, their guide John Cheney and some others went into the wilderness to look for streams that could be channeled to the works.

Cheney had borrowed Henderson's gun and returned it still cocked. By an isolated pond the gun went off accidentally, shooting Henderson in the chest. Cheney held him in his arms. "This is a terrible place for a man to die," said Henderson, and a few minutes later he died. The spot has been known ever since as Calamity Pond.

The town of Adirondac continued to grow for a while. The steel mill was finally built, in New Jersey. Adirondac iron was of high quality, but the iron in the ore was mixed with another mineral. It was hard and expensive to purify the ore, and there

*The ruins of the village of Adirondac, which stand to this day. (Photo courtesy the Adirondack Museum)*

was no way to get the iron out of the mountains cheaply. There was no coal to be found in the ancient rock, so the McIntyre mine used charcoal, which did not work as well, to melt the ore. In 1857 the mines closed down.

The busy village of Adirondac was abandoned. Twenty years later writer Charles Dudley Warner called its ruins "the most dismal spot in the mountains."

Yet it was one of the mine's problems that brought it to life again. The other mineral in the ore was titanium dioxide, one of the whitest pigments known. Other ore was better for iron, but the McIntyre mine was one of the few American sources of titanium. During World War II the mines were revived, a railroad was built and, until a few years ago, the mine produced titanium dioxide. Then it closed down once again. Today it is best known as a starting point for trails to the High Peaks. Off one of the most popular trails is Calamity Pond, where a monument to David Henderson still stands.

## Four. Explorers and Writers

THE McINTYRE MINE had one other part to play in the story of the Adirondacks. The first group to climb Mount Marcy started from there. This short trip was more than a first climb; it was a discovery. It started the stream of visitors who made the Adirondacks famous.

Until then nobody had known that the "dismal" Adirondacks boasted a mountain more than a mile high. Geographers thought that the Catskills were New York's highest mountains. Although iron forges and farms had sprung up near Whiteface Mountain, the peak was said to be only 2,600 feet above sea level. In 1836, while working on the New York State Geological Survey, geologist Ebenezer Emmons measured it at 4,855 feet.[1]

From the top of Whiteface Emmons had seen even higher mountains. Another scientist, William Redfield, had seen them, too, and had already planned to climb the highest. (As it was in Essex County, he called it the "High Peak of Essex.") The next

---

[1]Emmons was very close. Whiteface is 4,867 feet high.

year the two visited the McIntyre mine, hired John Cheney as a guide, and set off for the unexplored peak.

The party reached the top on August 5, 1837. All were surprised and overwhelmed by what they saw. John Cheney's description became famous:

> *It makes a man feel what it is to have all creation under his feet. There are woods there which it would take a lifetime to hunt over, mountains that seem shouldering each other to boost the one whereon you stand up and away, heaven knows where. Thousands of little lakes among them so light and clear. Old Champlain, though fifty miles away, glistens below you like a strip of white birch when slicked up by the moon on a frosty night, and the Green Mountains of Vermont beyond it fade and fade away until they disappear as gradually as a cold scent when the dew rises.*

Emmons sketched the view from the mountain top, torn between admiring its beauty and considering its geology. He renamed the "High Peak of Essex" Mount Marcy after William Marcy, the governor of New York, and named the second highest mountain Mount McIntyre, after the owner of the iron works. He called the entire central range the Adirondacks, believing it the name of an Indian tribe that had once lived there. (The word is usually translated as "bark-eater." It is probably Iroquois for "foreigner.")

It was a good time for the mountains to be discovered. The first world-famous American writer, James Fenimore Cooper, was writing novels about frontier life that were read on both sides of the Atlantic. New painters began to show pride in America's scenery, wilder and grander than European scenes. Americans were looking for landscapes and characters that they could think of as their own. And the great wilderness to the north was as American as could be.

*There were surely no American Indians around when Ebenezer Emmons and his party explored the Adirondacks, but the artist who illustrated his 1838 report could not resist putting one in; it made the scene seem more primitive.*

Travelers, writers and painters explored the mountains. Charles Fenno Hoffman, a writer and outdoorsman who had only one leg, hired John Cheney to guide him up Mount Marcy. When he realized that he could not make it he sat down and cried. But he continued his tour, wrote one of the first books on the mountains, and made up the "Indian name" for Mount Marcy — "Tahawus" — that many people use today.

These early visitors did not come for the wilderness. In fact, they found much of the Adirondacks — the wetlands and swamps, for example — frightening and ugly. They looked at mountain scenery or a beautiful lake the way they would look at a painting, and they loved scenery that fit their idea of what

*The painters and photographers of the Adirondacks often showed sunset or moonlit scenes like this one, with a lone visitor to make the view seem sadder and more romantic. (Seneca Ray Stoddard photo)*

America should look like. The views they treasured showed the visitors a romantic world of soft twilight and natural grandeur.

The visitors also "discovered" the pioneer spirit they had read about in novels. Cooper's most popular books had a woodsman hero, Natty Bumppo, who knew as much forest lore as any Indian. To Hoffman, John Cheney was Natty Bumppo come to life. The Adirondacks were the unspoiled America, and guides like Cheney were the unspoiled Americans. They always told the truth, they knew all the secrets of the forest, they were brave without thinking about it and they never boasted. They were as strong as the mountains and as pure as the streams.

The settlers had been forced to fish and hunt to survive. Now their skills began to make them money. Some became guides, and others built hotels. The shrewdest of all, Paul Smith, built a small kingdom of hotels, lodges, and private camps that finally included its own power dam and electric railroad.

But that was yet to come. The writers and painters of the 1840s and 1850s were pioneers, in a way. The flood of tourists

*"Adirondack" Murray's savage trout. This picture, typical of Murray's exaggerations, inspired one of the funniest pieces of Adirondack writing, Charles Dudley Warner's "A Fight with a Trout," in which the fish is so strong it spins the fishing boat around like a whirlpool.*

started in 1869, when a Boston minister named William H. H. Murray published a book called *Adventures in the Wilderness*. After "Adirondack" Murray the mountains were changed forever.

Murray's book was filled with advice. He had lists of recommended supplies and good shops for fishing tackle and camping goods. He told his readers what hotels were good and whose pancakes were worth eating, where to hire a guide and what all this would cost.

That was not all. After this information came ten dazzling chapters of hunting and fishing stories. Murray claimed he had caught the biggest fish, shot the biggest deer and braved the highest waterfalls. His Adirondacks were a wonderland of nature, a true paradise.

People were eager to believe him. America was changing very quickly. The Civil War had been long and terrible, but it had helped turn the United States into a great industrial nation. Its fast-growing cities were large and noisy. Workers for the new factories lived in slums thrown together by greedy landlords or in shacks they made themselves. Coal smoke, wood smoke and horse manure covered buildings and streets. People were looking for an escape.

Murray's book, especially its adventure tales, showed Americans a world they thought they had lost. Thousands of readers started north in the summer of 1869, eager to see this paradise for themselves.

It was a wet summer that year, and the swarms of tiny, biting black flies, which are always bad, were worse than usual. The little hotels did not have beds for all the visitors, and there were many more tourists than guides. For some of the tourists the summer was a disaster. They went home furious at having been among "Murray's fools." "Murray was a liar," they said.

Part of the charge was true. Murray had tried to separate fact from fiction, but he had not tried very hard. One story told how he and guide "Honest John" Plumley went over "Phantom Falls" in a boat. (The boat was smashed, but Murray and "Honest John" survived.)

There are no "Phantom Falls" in the mountains. Many readers decided that Murray meant Buttermilk Falls on the Raquette River, which nobody could possibly survive. Murray never actually said that he *had* gone over Buttermilk Falls. But he never said that he *hadn't*.

Most of his readers, though, didn't care. They wanted to believe in the Phantom Falls and the Lost Pond that was "boiling with trout," and they loved what they found in the mountains — black flies and all. The newspapers made fun of the bug-bitten tourists, but thousands forgot or ignored the discomfort. The hotel owners built more rooms. Railroad men began to think of running tracks into the mountains. In just a few years the Adirondacks became the most fashionable summer resort area in America. The region's golden age had begun.

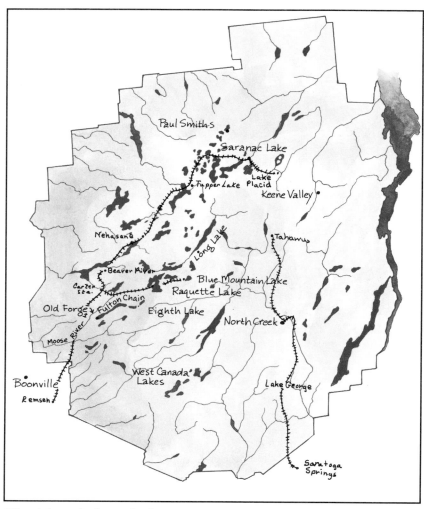

*The Adirondacks in the late 1800s.*

## Five. Tourists and Guides

"MURRAY'S FOOLS" had found a few hotels and a handful of guides. Most of them travelled west from Lake Champlain to the Saranac and St. Regis lakes. They stayed at Martin's Hotel or at Paul Smith's, and they hired guides to help them fish for trout and hunt deer along the lakes and rivers of the central Adirondacks.

Ten years later tens of thousands of visitors came. From the west they followed the Moose River valley to the Forge House on the Fulton Chain of lakes. From the southeast they took the railroad to North Creek and rode in stagecoaches and buckboards to the new hotels at Blue Mountain Lake. Guides worked at all the hotels, struck bargains with tourists and took them off for one or two weeks in the wild.

The outdoors writer George Washington Sears, who signed his books "Nessmuk," visited the western lakes from 1880 to 1883. His train stopped at Boonville, north of Utica. He described the road from Boonville to the first hotel, at Moose River, as 12 miles of "hills, hollows, sand up to the hub, boulders, and corduroy road" (a "road" made of logs laid crosswise in the mud). It was so rough that Nessmuk packed his canoe in straw and held it on the wagon by hand. The road to the Forge House was even worse. One year he carried his canoe 13 miles on his back rather than ship it by carriage.

*A postcard view of the Chain from the Forge House, Old Forge, N.Y., much as Nessmuk saw it. (Photo courtesy the Adirondack Museum)*

The shores of the Fulton Chain were already sprouting "camps." Some of them were open lean-tos, but others were real summer homes. Nessmuk was able to find wilderness when he wanted, but it was already gone from Blue Mountain Lake. "It has often been called the gem of the wilderness," he complained. "But its days of natural wildness are gone forever. There are three large hotels on its banks filled to overflowing with guests. Lines of stages leave daily for different points."

This was in 1880. More was to come. In 1882 the huge Prospect House, with room for 500 guests, was built on Blue Mountain Lake. Its owners boasted that it was the first electrically-lit hotel in the world. Thomas Edison himself had installed the generator. A guidebook listed all its attractions:

> *For amusement are billiard rooms, bowling alleys, tennis grounds, golf links, broad boats and narrow Adirondack skiffs. Saddle horses and livery outfits can be had. Music is had afternoons and evenings.*

[ 32 ]

And in case you found all the sports and concerts in the wilderness a little hectic, the Prospect House had "a large cottage removed some distance from the main building" for "guests who may wish for greater quiet."

*The lavish Prospect House in Blue Mountain Lake. The two-story outhouse is to the left. (Seneca Ray Stoddard photo courtesy the Chapman Historical Museum)*

The Prospect House was a little piece of the city in the clean mountain air, although it lacked a few modern touches. There was no plumbing. Guests used a two-story outhouse. There was no railroad to Blue Mountain Lake, so every guest and all the machinery had to be carried 38 miles from North Creek in coaches or buckboards. The Adirondack Stage Company took seven and a half painful, bumpy hours to make the trip.

This palace in the wilderness was part of one family's Adirondack empire. Thomas Clark Durant had made a fortune building the Union Pacific Railroad to California. Now he began running railroads through the Adirondacks while his sons built hotels and private camps around Raquette Lake and Blue Mountain Lake.

On Raquette Lake one son, William West Durant, built Camp Pine Knot. It was the first of a new kind of "camp": a group of buildings, almost like a small village, with different houses for sleeping, eating and partying. Other buildings housed servants and guests.

The fashion caught on quickly. Durant built "great camps" for the very wealthiest families in America. Around the camps the rich bought up large chunks of land for their own hunting and exploring.

To reach his camps and hotels Durant built a wonderfully complicated system of railroads and steamship lines. By 1900 you could take the Raquette Lake Railroad to a lakeside station. Steamers ran across the lake and up the Marion River. There you changed to the shortest full-sized railroad in the world — the Marion River Carry Railroad, which ran three-quarters of a

*Vacationers on a picnic excursion in the wilderness. (Seneca Ray Stoddard photo courtesy the Chapman Historical Museum)*

*An Adirondack lean-to, with trees chopped down all around to make the building and warm its occupants. (Seneca Ray Stoddard photo courtesy the Chapman Historical Museum)*

mile to Utowana Lake. Then you boarded another steamer to Blue Mountain Lake.

Men still came to the mountains for hunting and fishing. Their families usually stayed behind in the camps and hotels, although the more daring women joined them or even went off on their own in full skirts and button shoes.

Around the popular hotels deer and trout were already scarce. This was a problem, since every visitor wanted to return to the city with a trophy to prove his skill at hunting or fishing. By 1880 the state was stocking "wild" lakes with bass and other popular fish. The deer grew wiser and shyer. One guide claimed he had to hold the deer by the tail so the "sportsmen" could get close shots, and that even then some of them missed.

The would-be hunters and fishermen hired a guide to take them into the wilderness. When they reached an attractive spot the visitors sat around while the guide unloaded the packs, often heavy with fine wine and dress clothing, made dinner and built a lean-to or "open camp." Watching the guide build a lean-to was a part of the vacation.

The Adirondack lean-to had three walls and was open at the front. Young trees were cut for a frame and bark was peeled off trees to make the walls and ceiling. The guide then wove fresh balsam boughs into a soft and fragrant bed and felled a few large logs, which burned all night in front of the camp to keep away the bears, black flies and evening chill.

For many visitors the real wilderness experience was a week with an Adirondack guide. Murray's book and hundreds of others had made the Adirondack guide famous. Men paid high prices to say they had been guided by Mitchell Sabattis, Alvah Dunning or "Old Mountain" Phelps.

The "sport," his guide (manning the oars), and the sport's trophy in an Adirondack guideboat. (Photo courtesy the Adirondack Museum)

There were many types of guides. The Long Lake guides were famous hunters and boatmen and helped develop the beautiful Adirondack guideboat, a fast, light, oared boat pointed at both ends — a cross between a rowboat and a canoe. It was big enough for the guide and his customers but light enough for the

*Mitchell Sabattis, late in life. (Seneca Ray Stoddard photo courtesy the Chapman Historical Museum)*

guide to take on his shoulders over the many "carries" between lakes. (The guides never called them "portages.") Fast and maneuverable, the Adirondack guideboat was one of the finest small boats ever designed.

In 1880 the 80-year-old Abenaki Indian Mitchell Sabattis was still the most famous Long Lake guide. He was small, quiet, and so strong that he worked as a guide into his nineties. He could track a deer at night by the sound of its footsteps, with a rifle in one hand and a lantern in the other. His hotel was not as fancy or as famous as the Prospect House, but visitors looking for the "real" Adirondacks stayed there whenever they could. After he died, in 1906, a mountain to the east of Long Lake village was named after him, and a village to the west was given his name.

Sabattis was both a woodsman and a gentleman. Another guide, Alvah Dunning, who lived on Raquette Lake, was a fine woodsman but one of the toughest characters around. He preferred to be alone. In fact, he was really more of a hermit than a guide. When he felt crowded at Raquette Lake he moved a few miles to Eighth Lake. When tourists began to "discover" that lake, in the 1890s, Alvah went west to the Rockies. He was 83. Soon he was back, tired and sad. He died three years later.

*Arpad Gerster's portrait of Alvah Dunning.*

Alvah Dunning never cared for money, or company, or anything but the woods. He had a low opinion of the people who hired him:

> *They pay me well enough, but I'd rather they stay out o' my woods. They come, and I might as well guide 'em as anybody, but I'd ruther they'd stay ter hum and keep their money. I don't need it. I kin git along without 'em. They're mostly durned fools, anyhow!*

But Dunning was as sentimental as he was surly. He had dropped his old silver watch overboard while fishing, and one of the summer visitors in the area, Dr. Arpad Gerster, etched a

*"Old Mountain" Phelps became a tourist attraction in himself. Seneca Ray Stoddard, who took this picture of the guide, suggested to tourists that they visit Phelps at his home, "for a cordial welcome and a pleasant hour is certain to be the result." (Photo courtesy the Adirondack Museum)*

portrait of Dunning that perfectly captured his sharp-edged looks. Dr. Gerster sold enough proofs to buy a gold watch and got William West Durant to give the watch to Dunning at Christmas. The old man fainted with delight.

The High Peaks area to the east was less popular than the lake country, but it, too, had its guides. None was more famous than Orson "Old Mountain" Phelps from Keene Valley. Phelps was short, bow-legged and bearded. His voice was a high-pitched squeak. He was talkative, lazy (some said), got lost every now and then, and never took orders. His clients did not care. They hired him to hear him talk and to share his overwhelming love for the mountains.

The mountains were Old Mountain Phelps's truest friends, and he loved them the way others love their spouse or children.

Mount Marcy he called "Old Mercy" and once, after a long absence, his party saw him throw himself at its sides, hugging it. The Opalescent River was "Miss Opalescent" — too pretty, he said, to be anything but a young girl. He loved to tell of standing on Indian Head, looking over Lower Ausable Lake, with a great circular rainbow all around him ". . . only at one place there was an indentation in it, where it rested on the lake, just enough to keep it from rolling off."

He had no patience with those who didn't appreciate his mountains. He once guided two women to the top of Marcy. At once they fell to talking. "Why, there they were," recalled Phelps, "right before the greatest view they ever *saw*, talkin' about the *fashions!* I was a great mind to come down, and leave 'em there."

On another trip he refused to build a camp on the south shore of Upper Ausable Lake, with its wonderful view of the triple-peaked mountain he had helped name Gothics. His clients complained that on the north shore there was no view. But that was Phelps's point: you had to keep the view special. "Waal now," he argued, "them Gothics ain't the kinder scenery yer want ter *hog down!*" The camp was built on the north shore.

Phelps was so in love with the Adirondacks that he began to write poetry and articles about them. But today we remember instead the mountain names he helped coin: Haystack, Basin, Saddleback, Gothics, and Skylight. This odd mix of names — plain, fancy, poetic — seems to say everything about Old Mountain Phelps.

Not everybody came to the mountains to visit. Some came to stay. From the early days the Adirondacks had boasted a few hermits. The most famous one came with the early tourists and lumbermen. Louis Seymour, or "Adirondack French Louie," left Quebec with a travelling circus and came to the West Canada Lakes, in the west-central mountains, in 1868. After making winter runs with a few trappers he decided to live on his own. In

1873 he settled down by West Lake, where he trapped, hunted, fished and worked out his own way of life.

He was a friendly hermit, although he would wash for nobody and wouldn't stand for calendars. "Around here," he insisted, "one day is just like the others." He stacked frozen trout in a shed to last him through the winter. In the spring he buried the rotting leftovers in his garden. The smell was horrible, but his vegetables grew huge and sweet.

Louie believed in his fertilizer, but he believed even more in snakes. They ate the potato bugs, he insisted, and to attract them he built snake houses — long pieces of wood propped up on stones — and set out food. In time the snakes were so well trained that Louie could call them by pounding on a stump. They would slither out and Louie would toss them food. Louie's cabin is gone now, but his pets' descendants still live around West Lake.

Every winter Louie would come into town to sell his furs and get drunk. He would spend a week or so on a tremendous binge and then leave, making all the innkeepers happy. But he planned his binges well. He always left money with a friend, so he never went back to his cabin broke. And from one binge to the next he drank no alcohol. Life alone required a sober head.

In time "French Louie" became a familiar figure around the West Canadas. He died in 1915, and the schools closed to let the children go to his funeral.

The most important settler of the golden age was neither farmer, guide, hotel-keeper nor hermit. Dr. Edward Livingston Trudeau came to Paul Smith's hotel in the 1870s, dying of tuberculosis. Forty years later, when the disease finally beat him, he was world-famous, and nearby Saranac Lake was a world center for tuberculosis treatment.

It is hard now to imagine what tuberculosis meant in those days. Like AIDS today, it was a disease nobody expected to survive. But many more people suffered from it. Everyone had

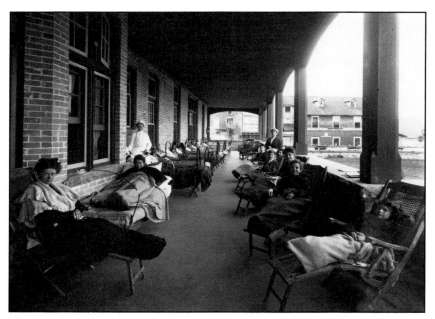

*Women and children taking the "cure" in an early sanatorium.*
*(Photo courtesy the Lake Placid Center for the Arts)*

friends or relatives who had died from it.

Trudeau came from a wealthy New York City family. His brother had died of tuberculosis, but Edward continued a happy if wasteful life until he found out that he, too, had taken sick.

There had been other "consumptives" in the Adirondacks. Murray's book had told of one miraculous cure, and many desperate people had tried to repeat the miracle. Few were able to. Trudeau knew of the stories but went to Paul Smith's with no real hope. He only wanted to die where he had been happiest. When he got there in the spring of 1873 the guide who carried him to his room found him "no heavier than a dried lambskin."

A few months of rest, hunting and good food gave him new energy, and Trudeau returned to New York. The next year his illness was worse than ever, and he came back. On the advice of a friend who believed strongly in rest and fresh air, Trudeau

*These children had tuberculosis or had parents with the disease. For them the cure was a "fresh air school" — outdoor games in all weather and unheated classrooms with open windows. (Photo courtesy the Adirondack Collection, Saranac Lake Free Library)*

spent the winter in the mountains. This seemed to work. In 1876 he moved to Saranac Lake. He lived there until his death in 1915.

Trudeau had not planned to practice medicine again. But he could not turn away from the sick. In 1884 he built a tiny cottage, "Little Red," for his first tuberculosis patients. Soon it became the Adirondack Cottage Sanitarium, and later the Trudeau Sanatorium. Trudeau nursed his patients and studied tuberculosis.

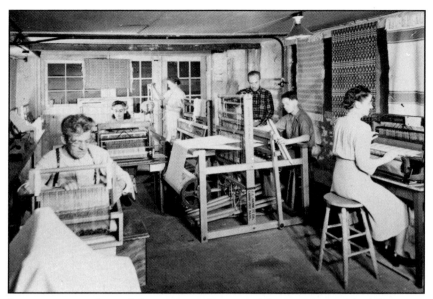

*Learning a trade and doing something useful was also part of the cure. (Photo courtesy the Adirondack Collection, Saranac Lake Free Library)*

The "cure" at Saranac Lake was rest, fresh air and, little by little, exercise. Nobody knows even today if the cure really worked. Many of Trudeau's patients died. But quite a few lived, many more than had survived other treatments. Soon Saranac Lake was filled with sanatoria, and the Trudeau model was being imitated throughout the United States.

Trudeau's sanatorium charged its patients only five dollars a week, when nearby hotels cost four dollars a day. The doctor made constant visits to old friends in New York to raise money. His patients loved him. He treated them like children but wanted them to "grow up" with a sense of power over their terrifying disease. Almost all looked back at their stays with happiness. Many stayed in Saranac Lake after their cure. With very few exceptions the people of the town accepted the sick, served their needs, and never turned away from them.

Tuberculosis slowly lost its power. We do not know why, but by the 1930s the Saranac Lake sanatoria were emptying. In 1952 a drug was found that cured the disease, and two years later the Trudeau Sanatorium closed down. The research center stayed open, but nobody needed the cure any more. Drugs were faster and surer.

In Saranac Lake, though, and in Edward Trudeau, the Adirondacks had given the world a lesson in treating the sick with dignity and decency. It was the most golden part of the golden age.

*For these tuberculosis patients the sanatorium was probably the most beautiful and interesting place they had ever lived in. They are patients at Ray Brook, New York State's public sanatorium, for those who could not afford private care. (Photo courtesy the Adirondack Collection, Saranac Lake Free Library)*

*To make charcoal for their forges early Adirondack iron works used kilns like these. This was one of the earliest uses for Adirondack trees, and around the forges stretched acres of bare hillsides. (Photo courtesy the New York State Archives)*

## Six. The Loggers

WHEN THE TOURISTS crowded around the Fulton Chain and Blue Mountain Lake and young ladies were common climbers on Mount Marcy, long-time visitors complained that the wilderness was getting too crowded. The Adirondacks were being ruined, they complained. They were right. But the tourists were not to blame. The great Adirondack wilderness was being destroyed by logging.

The tall pines along lakes George and Champlain had been cut down long before, and around the small iron works trees were felled for charcoal. But the heart of the Adirondacks was safe for many years. In the 1700s logs were floated to market in great rafts. This did not work on the narrow, twisting Adirondack streams. In 1813, though, loggers realized that they could send loose logs downstream on the spring flood. This new way of shipping logs changed the industry. It opened up all of the Adirondack forests and made New York the greatest lumbering state in the country.

*A logging camp in the snow, around the end of the nineteenth century. (Photo courtesy the New York State Archives)*

Waves of loggers moved through the mountains, taking more trees each time. First to go were the pines, the best wood for building. Then came the hemlocks' turn. Tanneries used the tannin from hemlock bark to turn animal skins into leather. They stripped the bark from the trees and left the rest to rot.

Finally, after the Civil War, loggers began supplying the paper mills along the Hudson River, the Black River and Lake Champlain. Paper mills, unlike builders, could use any size tree. This wave of loggers cleared entire mountainsides of spruce, fir and other evergreens for "pulpwood."

As long as the logs were carried by water the hardwood trees were safe. They were too heavy to float well. When the railroads began to cross the mountains, though, the maple, beech and other hardwoods began to fall.

Shipping logs by water gave the Adirondack logger's year a special rhythm. The mountain streams had the most water in early spring, when the snow melted, so the summer was spent

*A log chute in summer. In winter it will be a skidway. (Photo from the Apperson Collection of the Adirondack Research Center)*

cutting small pulpwood for the paper mills. The big trees were cut during the long winter and piled by the frozen streams. Many loggers farmed during the warm weather and with the first snows said goodbye to their families and walked 20 or more miles to a logging camp.

The loggers lived through the winter in these rough camps filled with bedbugs and the smoke of leaky wood stoves. They felled trees with axes or two-handled saws. The trimmed-off branches and thin tops, or "slash," was left where it fell. The loggers cut the trees into 13-foot lengths, or "markets," and branded the logs like cattle — every lumber firm had its own mark.

Paths were cut to the very tops of mountains to slide the logs downhill. Heaps of straw or evergreen boughs smoothed the paths and snow was packed over the boughs. Fifty or more logs at a time were chained together and pulled down these "skidways" by horses or oxen. It was hard work for animals and men. There was always the danger of "a ride down the mountain," a runaway load. Then the terrified loggers and their animals

*A load of logs on a horse cart. (Photo courtesy the New York State Archives)*

*Logs going through a dam on one of the last log drives in the High Peaks, in the 1930s. (Photo from the Apperson Collection of the Adirondack Research Center)*

could do nothing but try to get out of the way.

Winter work ran around the clock. One logger remembers:

> *We used to have breakfast about one in the morning. We'd go out and load logs soon after one a.m. and get our round loaded by about five a.m., with three or four gangs of loaders. Then we'd haul. We'd be back in camp, eat again, and go in the bunkhouse. Maybe raise hell for a little while, or maybe go to bed about nine or 9:30. Then the first team would start coming back. As soon as the horses were fed, they'd get you up. 'Course, a lot of times we were loading at nine or ten o'clock at night, too. We'd be out there with lanterns in the morning and we were there with lanterns at night.*
> *I think loading we got 70 cents a day — 50 cents if you were cutting.*

*Loggers camped out in a lean-to. (Photo courtesy the New York State Archives)*

Many lumber camps built low dams and piled the logs up in the "flowed lands" behind them. The spring runoff made a lake and floated the whole field. Other logging dams gave an extra rush of icy water to float the logs over rapids and waterfalls.

The river drivers who worked the logs downstream were the best-paid and bravest men in the camp. The wild spring runoff tossed the logs in every direction. Only the strongest, most nimble drivers could keep up. They followed the logs downstream for days, often without sleep. They kept the logs moving along with their long "peavy hooks," metal hooks on poles. If all went well the logs would be carried to the mills many miles away.

But things did not always go well. The logs often jammed up, and the river drivers had to climb over the jam and free the logs. This was the most dangerous of all lumbering jobs. First the drivers tried to pick the jam apart. Usually one log was the key to the mess. They chopped away this "jackstraw" and hoped that the jam would work itself out — but slowly, so they could reach the bank before the hundreds of tons of logs rushed downstream again.

If that failed they placed dynamite among the logs and blew the jam apart. Many men were washed away, crushed by the logs or killed in the explosions.

The biggest mills were in Glens Falls, north of Albany, where a huge log fence was thrown across the Hudson every spring.

*A log jam. (Photo courtesy the New York State Archives)*

The logs were stopped at this "boom" and the lumberjacks sorted them out by brand mark. In the 1870s over a million logs piled up behind the Big Boom every spring.

A million trees seems like a lot, but the forests were so great that for a long time nobody noticed the devastation. In 1869, in *Adventures in the Wilderness*, Murray claimed that the Adirondacks were far better than the Maine woods. Maine had the signs of the lumbermen everywhere, he said, but in the Adirondacks the mountains were untouched.

This was not true. When Murray's book came out there had been logging in the central Adirondacks for twenty years. Almost all of the High Peaks were cut sooner or later. In all, only about one-tenth of the forest escaped the ax.

Lumber companies bought land cheaply from the state, cut everything they could find, and then stopped paying taxes. The ruined land went back to state ownership. For pennies an acre the state sold good timbering land. A few years later it got back a wasteland of stumps and scrap.

Many lumber companies didn't even bother buying the land. Hundreds of thousands of dollars of timber were stolen from state land every year. Once a tree has been cut down, of course, there is no way to tell where it has come from.

There are ways of cutting trees that keep the forest growing. But few Americans thought about that in the 1800s. The Adirondack logging companies did not. They were out for a fast dollar, and they didn't care about the future. They cut every tree they could reach, and this "clear-cut" forest was ready for disaster.

The useless branches and leaves, or "slash," that was left behind dried in the sun and became a terrible fire hazard. In the Adirondacks much of the soil is made up of dead twigs and leaves. This "duff" catches fire easily. Fires that started in the slash burned the very soil away.

Water was as big a threat as fire. The dead trees no longer

*The result of a forest fire. (Photo courtesy the New York State Archives)*

held the soil in place. The rains and melting snow washed the soil into streams that once ran clear. Now they churned muddy brown in the spring and dried up in the summer.

Soon voices were being raised against the loggers. The first "environmentalists" had already appeared, although they were not called that. In 1864 a diplomat and traveller named George Perkins Marsh had written a book called *Man and Nature*. He used examples from the Middle East and Europe, showing that whole countries could be destroyed if people wasted their forests and rivers. He pointed to the Huang Ho, or Yellow River, in China. It had once been a clear stream, flowing through rich forests. After the forests were cut down the river became muddy and uncontrollable, flooding almost every year and killing thousands of people. The floods washed away topsoil and ruined millions of peasant farms. Destroying the forest had created a wasteland.

People who read Marsh's book saw the same thing happening in the Adirondacks. They worried about the Hudson and Mohawk rivers and the Erie Canal, which were all fed by Adirondack water. If the Adirondacks went the way of the Chinese forests, New York State might lose the water routes that made it wealthy. The citizens of New York began to talk of an Adirondack Forest Preserve.

## Seven. Forever Wild

IN 1857, JUST TWENTY YEARS after Emmons climbed Mount Marcy, a writer and lawyer named Samuel H. Hammond saw the loggers and settlers starting to push through the mountains. He wondered where he would be able to go "to find the woods, the wild things, the old forests, and hear the sounds which belong to nature." He made a suggestion that must have seemed crazy: "Had I my way," he wrote, "I would mark out a circle of a hundred miles in diameter, and throw around it the protecting aegis [shield] of the constitution. I would make it a forest forever. It should be a misdemeanor to chop down a tree, and a felony to clear an acre…"

Something very much like Hammond's idea has become the law for the state lands. But in 1857 it was only a dream. Hammond knew what most people would say, and he put their reply into his book:

*Can you grow corn on these hills? Can you harness these rivers to great waterwheels, or make reservoirs of these lakes? Can you convert these old forests into lumber? Can you coin them into dollars?*

It seemed un-American to leave land uncleared and timber uncut. America was a practical country, and an Adirondack preserve did not seem practical.

*One of Verplanck Colvin's survey parties. (Photo courtesy of Mrs. Thomas Hobbie, Sodus, N.Y., née Elizabeth Morgan)*

Eleven years after Hammond's book and one year before Murray's, a young man named Verplanck Colvin made a speech at Lake Pleasant in the southern part of the region. He proposed "an Adirondack Park or timber preserve." His speech may have seemed as crazy as Hammond's book, but Colvin did more than dream. He made his dream come true.

Verplanck Colvin came from a wealthy Albany family and was trained as a lawyer. In 1865, when he was 18, he had made his own map of the mountains and had surveyed part of the map himself. That map changed his life. Surveying the Adirondacks, and telling others about them, became his life's work.

In 1870 Colvin climbed Mount Seward, near Saranac Lake. He was the first man known to have done so, and the State Museum published the story of his climb. The story ended with another plea for an "Adirondack park or timber preserve. . . .

*One of Colvin's own illustrations, showing a boat lost in the ice of a newly discovered lake. The boatmen survived — "shivering, wet, icy and weary," wrote Colvin.*

The interests of commerce and navigation," said Colvin, "demand that these forests should be preserved."

Colvin visited the State Capitol, spoke to everyone he could find, and in 1872 got himself appointed chief of an Adirondack survey. For the next thirty years he travelled back and forth across the mountains. He wrote a report every year. The survey was never finished, but by the time Colvin was fired by an impatient legislature the Adirondack Park was a reality.

Colvin's reports were important weapons in the fight. They had pages of numbers and maps, like most reports; but they were also readable and exciting. Colvin made surveying into an adventure, and his books are full of stories. Much of the land he surveyed was still unexplored. In his first trip Colvin discovered the highest source of the Hudson, a tiny lake on the side of Mount Marcy. He gave it the wonderfully poetic name of Lake Tear-of-the-Clouds.

His discoveries were only part of the adventure. Colvin had a genius for getting into trouble. Over and over he would stay too long on the tops of mountains and have to climb down at night. On August 17, 1873, he and his party climbed Dix, the seventh-highest peak in the Adirondacks. Early in the afternoon they reached the top, and hours of survey work followed as they located other mountains and lakes.

> *Absorbed in our work* [Colvin reports], *we were startled by sunset. It would be impossible to descend in the dark, amid the cliffs and ledges, and our camp and camp-guard and provisions were miles away. There was no time for discussion and I ordered a descent into Hunter's Pass, to find water and a resting place. Water, unfortunately, was not to be found, and soon we became entangled amid ledges, slides, and cavernous rocks. In the darkness, clinging by roots, aiding each other from ledge to ledge, we finally found ourselves slipping on the edge of rocks draped in cold, wet moss, and a little lower we found water!*
>
> *A moment's rest and we descended further only to find we were in a cul-de-sac — with walls of air — the verge of an overhanging cliff, so high that even the tree-tops below were not distinguishable. The slender stream leapt the edge and was lost in the depths. Here we were compelled to halt, and passed the night.*[2]

This was a common story with Colvin; in that same report he listed "the most *noteworthy* night descents" as "Wallface mountain, Mt. Colden, Mt. Dix, Mt. Marcy, Mt. MacIntyre, Blue mountain, Graves mountain, etc., etc., etc."

---

[2]Colvin's language is very fancy, in the fashion of his day, and this quote has been edited. All the words, however, are his own.

*Another of Colvin's pictures, showing the signalling station he built on the summit of Mount Marcy.*

Colvin liked to begin in the late summer and work through the fall; it was easier to take sightings when the leaves were off the trees. Thanks to his special talent for trouble, he would often end up trekking through terrifying snowstorms. In some of his reports Colvin sounds like an arctic explorer, stumbling through snowstorms with no food, his brave crew barely rescuing their boats from sinking in ice-covered ponds.

Like Emmons before him, Colvin could never decide between his love of the wilderness and his concern for science. When Colvin describes his "stan-helio" — a tower capped with tin sheets, which reflected the sun and made a perfect sighting-point — he is as excited as when he describes the view from a mountain. He invented a collapsible canoe and wrote pages praising it. When wilderness got in the way of his surveying, wilderness always lost. His crew cleared entire mountaintops to improve the sightlines. They chopped down more than two acres of forest on Ampersand Mountain in 1873. Its summit is still bare.

Besides adventure stories, Colvin's reports were filled with ideas for making the Adirondacks useful. He saw them as a "forest-farm and source of timber." He suggested canals linking all the major Adirondack lakes, so "a single mind at the Capitol may control by telegraph the flow of rivers, and at the tap of a key turn many million cubic feet of water from the St. Lawrence to the Mohawk River, the Hudson, or to Lake Champlain." Colvin even proposed a huge dam on the upper Hudson. Entire valleys would be flooded to supply water to New York City. Most important of all, though, was the "watershed." Only an Adirondack forest, Colvin insisted, could store up winter snows and spring rain and run-off. Only an Adirondack Park could ensure a steady flow of water to New York State's canals and rivers.

Colvin's park would not be a very wild place. But America was a practical, business-minded country, and wilderness still seemed like something that needed to be cleared and settled. The friends of the Adirondacks were businessmen, led by the New York Board of Trade and Transportation. They loved the woods, but they needed good, practical reasons to save them — reasons that made business sense. Colvin's reports gave them those reasons.

By the early 1880s, thanks to Colvin's reports, the Adirondacks had become a major issue. Meetings were held in New York City. Speakers pointed to Colvin's reports and to Marsh's *Man and Nature*. Uncontrolled logging, they argued, would ruin the climate, dry up the Hudson River and the Erie Canal, and put an end to New York's wealth. The watershed had to be protected, they continued, even if logging had to be stopped.

The State Senate set up a special committee to recommend action. Its report, published in 1885, blamed timber thieves, lumbermen and railroads for turning the forests into an "unproductive and dangerous desert." The legislature did not want to offend the lumber companies, but it was worried about the watershed. It was afraid, too, of losing New York's last important source of wood. In May of 1885 it established an Adirondack Forest Preserve.

The Forest Preserve was a fancy name for all the state land in the Adirondack area. A Forest Commission was set up to look after these lands. Its rangers would prevent fires and keep timber thieves out. It was also supposed to rent the land to "scientific" lumbermen. The forests of Europe had long been managed to produce a steady supply of wood. Professional foresters were going to do the same with the Adirondacks.

It might have worked, although we would have ended up with a very different Forest Preserve. But the foresters were never given a chance. The Forest Commissioners had too many friends in the logging industry, and they let companies clear-cut the forests the way they had before. They did nothing to stop the timber thieves. The Forest Preserve was little more than a joke.

Even though the preserve was working badly, the legislature decided to extend it. The state lands were scattered all over the mountains. The Forest Commission suggested that the whole of the Adirondacks be called a park. They drew a map of this park in their 1891 report, marking the boundary in blue. In 1892 the state named this area the Adirondack Park, and ever since then the boundary has been called the "Blue Line." (The Blue Line has been redrawn several times. The original Park was less than half the size of today's.) But the Park, too, was something of a myth. The state hoped to buy and protect all the land and rent parts of it to campers. But it did nothing. Less than a fifth of the "Park's" land was state-owned Forest Preserve.

The very next year a new law allowed the Forest Commission to sell timber from any part of the Park. The people who had fought to protect the Adirondacks were furious. For almost ten years they had watched the state betray its fine words. The Forest Preserve was preserving nothing. The Adirondack Park

STOP THIEF!

*Years after the Park was formed, newspapers still showed the forest industry as timber thieves. (Cartoon from the* New York Herald, *April 20, 1903)*

was being sold to the lumbermen and their friends.

In 1894 there was a chance to change things. The state constitution was being rewritten. The New York constitution cannot be changed easily. The legislature has to pass an amendment. After a new legislature is elected the amendment has to

*Drowned forests like these inspired Judge William Goodelle to suggest that the preserve be protected from destruction by flooding. (Seneca Ray Stoddard photo courtesy the Chapman Historical Museum)*

pass again. Then the voters of the whole state have to approve the change. Constitutional protection was the best way, many people thought, to take the Adirondacks away from the legislature, the Forest Commissioners and their lumber company friends.

The Constitutional Convention was three-quarters over when a New York lawyer proposed that the constitution ban logging throughout the Forest Preserve. The idea was welcomed by everyone. Even the professional foresters liked it, for they disliked the Forest Commission. They hated clear-cut logging as much as anyone else and thought that their turn to harvest the Adirondacks would come in 1915, after the next constitutional convention.

There was only one change. A Syracuse judge, William

Goodelle, reminded the convention of the trees flooded and drowned in lumber company ponds. He asked that one word be added: the constitution should not let trees be sold, removed, or *destroyed*.

That one word saved much of the Adirondacks from being flooded. On January 1, 1895, the new constitution went into effect. Article Seven, Section Seven read:

> *The lands of the state, now owned or hereafter acquired, constituting the Forest Preserve as now fixed by law, shall be forever kept as wild forest lands. They shall not be leased, sold, or exchanged, or be taken by any corporation, public or private, nor shall the timber thereon be sold, removed, or destroyed.*

The Adirondacks — the state lands, at least — were now "Forever Wild." It sounded wonderful. But it took many years to decide what "Forever Wild" really meant.

## Eight. The Park Takes Shape

T HE "FOREVER WILD" SECTION has stayed in the
    New York Constitution ever since it was approved in 1894.
It is now Article Fourteen. Amendments have been passed
allowing a few dams, roads and ski trails, but the people have
defeated most attempts to weaken it.

Thanks especially to Judge Goodelle's addition, New York's
Forest Preserve has more protection than any other part of the
United States. Some cutting is allowed when trails are built or
maintained, but the rules are very strict. Even the fire observers,
some of whom spent the summer near the mountaintops, could
not cut trees down to feed their own wood stoves. In the middle
of the Adirondack forests they brought in non-Forest Preserve
wood to burn.

In the years just after the new constitution became law,
though, nobody really understood what "Forever Wild" meant.
Everyone realized that the lumber companies were out. But
most people also thought that the strict rules would last for only
a few years.

The Fisheries, Forest and Game Commission was sure
"Forever Wild" would be repealed. It drew up plans for logging

*Fighting a forest fire in the western Adirondacks in 1901. (Photo courtesy the New York State Archives)*

parts of the preserve. The new commissioners were interested in a healthy forest, since they planned to sell the wood some day. But they had as many friends in the lumber industry as the old commissioners had. Timber theft went on as before. The state did little to defend its land claims in court.

Worst of all, the commission did nothing to guard against forest fires. In 1903 more than 500 fires destroyed almost half a million acres of forest. Five years later, 300,000 more acres were burnt. Sparks from coal-burning locomotives started a third of these fires. The Forest, Fish and Game Commission (it had changed its name in 1900) reported that "the dead leaves, bushes, undergrowth, stumps, logs, and leafless trees" were so dry that "fires sprang up in the wake of nearly every train."

The few state rangers were no help. Louis Marshall, a famous lawyer, preservationist and social activist, wrote to the commission in disgust:

*The men who were designated to deal with these fires did
so by sitting in a boat, watching the flames as they drove
muskrats, mink, and other animals out of their holes, to
shoot the game which was driven out. The fire did not concern
them in any other way.*

In 1909 the legislature finally passed laws to reduce the danger
of fire. Coal-burning locomotives were banned during the summer, lumbermen had to trim slash, and six fire towers were built.
Soon more were added. Until the 1980s there were dozens of
towers throughout the Park, their lone observers searching for
smoke throughout the summer. Never again did the Adirondacks suffer from fires like those of 1903 or 1908.

*The fire tower on Hadley
Mountain, one of the last to
operate in the Adirondacks.
(Photo by Paul Steinberg)*

The trees were safe. But it was a very different forest than it
had been fifty years before. Fast-growing trees like paper birch,
the first trees to grow in a new forest, had taken the place of
spruce and hemlock in the burned-over areas. Many animals
had disappeared from the mountains. Eagles and falcons, wolves,
cougar, lynx and other predators had all vanished in the 1800s.

[ 69 ]

The hunters were partly to blame. But the changes people had made to the forest were as deadly as the hunters' bullets. The last moose in the Adirondacks was killed in the 1860s. The hunters, though, only finished what had been started by deer, for deer carry a parasite harmless to them but fatal to moose. Deer prefer clearings to deep forests. The clear-cut loggers and the farmers had left a good habitat for them, and people had killed off their natural predators, like the wolf. So the deer thrived, and the moose died.

The natural world of the Adirondacks was out of balance. It has taken many years to start restoring that balance. The first important step was to bring back the forest itself. Luckily, the forest rebuilds itself without our help. "Forever Wild" gave it the time it needed to grow back, and the Forest Commission gave it one giant helping hand. It brought back the beaver.

By the early 1800s the beaver was almost extinct in the Adirondacks. An 1894 law made killing them a crime. Pushed by the teen-aged outdoors writer Harry Radford, the state bought beaver and released them in the woods. By 1917 there were so many that one property owner tried to sue the state, claiming that the state-supported beaver had flooded his land. The state (and the beaver) won, and the beaver have flourished ever since.

They can still be a nuisance; beaver ponds have flooded trails and even roads. Only controlled trapping has kept them from taking over the Park. But few people doubt that their return was for the good. Their dams and ponds were an important part of the Adirondack cycle of life, and the forest was not complete without them.

There were other changes in those years. Many of them were hard on Adirondack people. The mountains fell out of fashion. The rich now spent their summers by the sea. The sea was closer to the eastern cities, railroad service was much better, and there was more to do than hunt and fish. Although Theodore

*Harry Radford, when he was leading the fight to restore the region's wildlife. (Illustration courtesy the Adirondack Museum)*

## Sweeping Legislative Victory!

**Woods and Waters' Black Bear Preservation Bill Becomes a Law.—Beaver Restoration Measure Passed Unanimously.—New Elk Bill Successful.**

*A cartoon from Radford's magazine, with all the animals he had helped reintroduce passing a resolution in his honor. Unfortunately, most of his reintroductions failed. Only the beaver, shown waiting his turn, flourished. (Illustration courtesy the Adirondack Museum)*

Roosevelt's family had summered near Paul Smith's, President Roosevelt built his summer home at Oyster Bay, on Long Island.

And the Adirondack vacation season is very short. The black flies bite into late June, and by late August the nights are cold. It is hard to support an expensive hotel on just two months' business. One by one the great resort hotels closed. The buildings were all wooden and most were lit by oil lamps; many burned, and few were rebuilt.

William West Durant's empire of railroads, hotels and great camps collapsed. Once he had entertained millionaires. By the early 1900s he had gone bankrupt, and he found a job as a hotel clerk in Long Lake.

*The rustic public room in a landed club. This club was the summer home of preservationist Louis Marshall and his sons Robert and George, the first "Forty-Sixers." (Photo courtesy the Adirondack Collection, Saranac Lake Free Library)*

As the hotels vanished something new appeared: the landed club. These clubs were started by groups of businessmen. They bought land for their own private hunting preserves and built huge but rustic clubhouses and guest houses. Soon after it was founded in 1890, the Adirondack League Club controlled more than 275 square miles near Old Forge. The club's lands, like many parks around the great camps, were logged by professional foresters. Game and fish were managed so that the visiting club members would have plenty to hunt and catch.

For many Adirondackers the golden years were over. There was still logging, of course, and woodworking at Tupper Lake, iron mining in the east and north and garnet mining at North Creek. But fewer people wanted guides. The clubs and tourist homes needed cooks and caretakers. These new jobs had none of the independence that guiding or farming had.

Visitors had once looked to the local people for the secrets of the woods. Now, with the clubs and the private parks taking over, the year-round people began to feel like strangers in their own homes. Their special knowledge and skills were no longer needed.

Worse than that, they could no longer travel or camp wherever they wanted. In the old days, when the Adirondacks were truly a wilderness, anyone could build a camp anywhere, chop down young trees for a lean-to frame, fell an old tree for a fire, and strip off bark for the walls and roof. Now the club lands and many of the timber lands were posted "No Trespassing." Guides and campers had to camp "on state," on the Forest Preserve lands. Only dead or downed timber could be used for fires, and it was against the law to cut trees and bark for a lean-to. The old-timers grumbled, and the visitors remembered sadly the smell of fresh bark and balsam.

That wonderful smell, though, had a very high price. Each new lean-to had been the center of a little clearing, a wound that had taken the forest years to heal. "Forever Wild" stopped this destruction. It forced everyone to treat the forest more gently. A new idea began to spread: the visitor to the wilderness should leave nothing behind but footprints.

Something was happening. A new Adirondack world was being created. The forests were growing back. New York spent millions of dollars buying land for the preserve; it grew from less than 700,000 acres in 1885 to almost 1,800,000 acres in 1919.

In 1919, after World War I, the Adirondacks were rediscovered. The new visitors came in a new invention, the automobile. Hikers and campers came not to hunt or play pioneer but to look for real wilderness. The "Forever Wild" section of the constitution had saved the mountains for all of the people of New York, and now the people came, more every year, to see them and to enjoy them, and perhaps to learn from them.

## Nine. Two Visions of the Adirondacks

IN 1919 THE CONSERVATION Commission changed its thinking about the Forest Preserve. For twenty-five years it had waited to start scientific forestry on the preserve, but its new commissioner, George D. Pratt, had different ideas. His 1919 report criticized lumbering, at least on the High Peaks. It spoke of the Adirondack Park's value as a vacation resort, a place for the nervous city dweller to relax, and it asked for a trail-building campaign, with guidebooks, maps and trailside shelters, to open up "this big vacation country."

Most of the High Peaks were then on private land. In some places hiking clubs had joined together to build and maintain trails, but there were no official trails on state land. The Conservation Commission had done nothing to encourage hikers.

There were forty-five fire towers in the Adirondacks, though, offering some of the best views in the mountains. Many hikers were already using the fire observers' trails. Now the state decided to connect these trails. It bought the summits of White-

*A "tourist court" from the early days of automotive tourism. (Photo courtesy the Adirondack Museum)*

face Mountain, Algonquin Peak, and mounts Seward and Marcy, not for timberlands but for the scenery. New York State was in the tourism business.

In 1920 the commission started its system of trails. Its workers marked the trails with colored metal disks nailed to trees, added turn-offs to especially good views, put up permanent lean-tos and opened roadside campgrounds. Most of this building was strictly illegal under "Forever Wild," but the commission believed that the tree-cutting was too little to worry about. It was more important that the people of New York be able to visit and enjoy their park.

The people came. By 1930 there were more than 400 miles of foot trails in the Forest Preserve, and a quarter of a million people spent at least a night at the new roadside campgrounds. In 1938 more than a million campers stayed overnight at the campsites, and thousands more stayed in the wilderness lean-tos. New roads, like one from Old Forge to Saranac Lake, brought millions into the heart of the mountains. The people had discovered their park.

The old reasons for coming to the Adirondacks, though, would not have attracted the new visitors. Hunting was now limited to one month in the fall, and over-fishing had put an end to the "lost" Adirondack fishing-holes that "boiled" with trout. The new Adirondacks had a different style — two different styles, in fact. Melvil Dewey and Robert Marshall gave the new visitors two very different pictures of the area.

Melvil Dewey invented the Dewey Decimal System for classifying books. He also had great talents as a businessman. On Mirror Lake, in the village of Lake Placid, he built the Lake Placid Club, the most famous of all Adirondack resorts. The club grew into two square miles of hotels, cottages, golf courses, tennis courts, schools and concert halls, with twenty-six farms to feed its members and its own fire department. Some people came to live year-round.

*Organized sports were an important part of life at the Lake Placid Club. This is the starting line for a hoop race, in front of the club's huge main building. (Photo courtesy the Lake Placid Center for the Arts)*

Melvil's son Godfrey realized that Lake Placid was a perfect spot for winter sports. He promoted ice skating, brought in teachers from Norway to teach skiing to the club members, and built a ski jump. In 1932 the club and the village became world-famous when they hosted the Winter Olympics. The dreaded Adirondack winter had become a new tourist season.

Many club members learned to love and understand the mountains and the wilderness. But Dewey had other reasons for building his club. He wanted only the "best" people around him. You had to be invited, and then prove that you were "better" than the ordinary person. Then you might become part of his group "of cultured people grouped with others of like tastes."

Like most other Adirondack club owners, Dewey kept out blacks, invalids and Jews. America grew less prejudiced but the club refused to change. It slowly faded away and finally closed for good. It left behind its vast clubhouse and a golf course. Its best monument is the Adirondack ski industry.

Robert Marshall was Jewish, so he would not have been admitted to the Lake Placid Club. But his influence on the Adirondacks was more meaningful and more lasting than Dewey's. Louis Marshall, Robert's father, a famous defender of civil rights as well as "Forever Wild," had a summer home on Lower Saranac Lake. The library there had a complete set of Colvin's reports, and Bob and his brother George read them eagerly. They longed to have adventures like Colvin's.

With the help and company of Herbert Clark, one of the last of the great Adirondack guides, the boys began climbing the High Peaks. Their first was Whiteface Mountain, which they climbed in 1918. Bob Marshall was seventeen and George was fourteen.

By 1920 or 1921 they had decided to climb all the peaks over 4000 feet high. They made up rules (the peaks had to rate as separate mountains) and came up with forty-two mountains. They climbed the last of them in 1922, when George was just

*The last scene of an outdoor production of "Rip Van Winkle" at the Lake Placid Club. (Photo courtesy the Lake Placid Center for the Arts)*

eighteen. Friends then suggested that they add the four peaks exactly 4000 feet high. The Marshalls agreed to this forty-six-mountain list, and in June, 1925, they and Herbert Clark climbed the last of them and became the first Adirondack "Forty-Sixers."[3]

The Marshall boys sometimes spent more than fifteen hours a day hiking and climbing. On one thirteen-day trip they climbed up a total of 50,000 feet — almost 10 miles, or up two Mount Everests.

---

[3]The maps the Marshalls used were not always accurate. Only forty-two of the forty-six peaks reach 4000 feet or more. To keep the rules the same, though, the Forty-Sixers (a mountain-climbing club) continue to use the Marshalls' list.

Their love of adventure soon deepened into a love of wilderness. The Marshalls made up another list, this one ranking the views from the forty-six mountain tops. Number one on the list was Mount Haystack. Haystack is the third-highest peak in New York, and its view of Mount Marcy is spectacular. Even more precious to Bob Marshall, though, was the fact that from Haystack he could see nothing but forests, mountains and lakes.

Absolute wilderness became Bob Marshall's ideal. It was valuable because it was something not made by people. Time in the wilderness gave people a chance to get outside the whole human world. They would return to the everyday world with a better sense of who they were and a clearer idea of what was important.

When Bob Marshall wrote about climbing the High Peaks others wanted to try climbing them. A church group from Troy, New York, started the Forty-Sixers, open to everyone who had made it up all forty-six. Another new organization, the Adirondack Mountain Club, promoted hiking and canoeing and joined older groups in watching over the Park. George Pratt, the former Conservation Commissioner, was its first president.

Many in these new organizations shared the Marshalls' love for wilderness. They saw that the forest's cycles of birth and death and decay had to be respected. They realized that the Adirondack Park is an entire ecosystem — a special community of plants and animals, different from the ones outside the Park. They tried to protect and rebuild that living world, supporting "Forever Wild" because it protects the entire Adirondack ecosystem, from arctic grasses to black bears.

The Adirondack Park is very big. For many years it seemed that there was room for everything and everyone: for clubs like Dewey's, for vacationers in their cars, for lovers of wilderness like the Marshalls, and for the plants and animals. New York State kept buying land, but it left the private landowners alone. A 1924 law banned billboards along the Park's roads. For almost

*Bob Marshall, guide Herbert Clark and George Marshall while they were climbing the High Peaks. (Photo courtesy the Adirondack Museum)*

fifty years the "signboard law" was the only rule that applied to the whole Park.

The Conservation Commission pushed for better roads and expanded its roadside campgrounds. A highway was built to the

*Commercial development in Lake George Village and the lake beyond.*
*(Photo © Alan Cederstrom; courtesy the Adirondack Council)*

top of Whiteface Mountain in 1927, so car-driving visitors
could sample a high-peaks view. The constitution had to be
changed to allow the road. Voters approved it as a memorial to
the veterans of World War One. There were forty-five other
High Peaks, after all, and the Forest Preserve was still growing.
It reached the 2,000,000-acre mark in 1952.

In 1949, near Whiteface Mountain, one of the first theme
parks in the United States was built. It was called Santa's Village. Other tourist attractions followed, many of them around
Lake George. In 1957 a superhighway, the Adirondack North-
way, began pushing through the eastern edge of the park. The
new roads and new attractions opened the Adirondacks up to
millions of new visitors. By 1967 two and a half million people
stayed overnight at the state campgrounds.

The Adirondacks were more popular than ever, and big real estate developers began to look at them. Here, they thought, was a perfect region for summer homes. More than half of it was private land. Hundreds of beautiful lakeshores and hillsides were for sale at the right price, all of them just a few hours by super-highway from cities like New York and Boston. Several companies made plans to build huge resort communities in the heart of the mountains.

But now people began to realize that there was not enough room. Development was eating away at the Park's open space. Once-lovely streets were now rows of hamburger stands and motels. Lake George Village, in particular, was full of "tourist traps," and new buildings in Lake Placid blocked the view of Mirror Lake and the mountains.

The developers were not the only ones to blame. The Park, someone said, was being loved to death. Thousands of hikers and campers were wearing away the trails and stomping over the rare alpine plants on the High Peaks summits. Some worried that the Park would become a few plots of over-hiked forest surrounded by cheap "attractions." By 1967 even New York's governor, Nelson Rockefeller, was wondering how it could be saved.

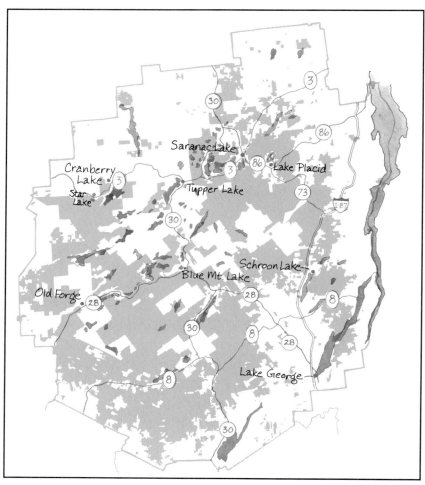

The Adirondacks today, showing Forest Preserve (shaded areas).

## Ten. Hard Decisions

ON JULY 29, 1967, Laurance Rockefeller, the governor's brother, released a report on the Adirondacks. He suggested giving the central part of the region to the federal government for an Adirondack National Park.

Almost everyone was against the plan. A quarter of the proposed national park was private land. The people who lived there were furious; they said the governor's brother wanted to run them off their own land. Hunters were mad, because there is no hunting in the national parks. Preservationists were just as angry. National parks are not protected by anything like the "Forever Wild" clause. They wondered how wild the national park would be, and they worried about the land left out of the new park.

The governor decided to name a Temporary Study Commission to make suggestions about the future of the Adirondacks. He appointed Harold K. Hochschild to it, and Hochschild became its leader.

Hochschild was a wealthy businessman who spent his spare time near Blue Mountain Lake. He was also a great student of the Adirondacks. He had written a history of the Blue Mountain Lake area and had founded the Adirondack Museum, one of the finest regional history museums in the world. His love and knowledge of the Adirondacks and his great political skill made the commission work.

Hochschild and the commission thought deeply about the

area and about the needs of the people who live there. They came up with a plan that tried to make room for both nature and people, and Hochschild and others pushed it through in 1971.

An Adirondack Park Agency, or APA, was set up to guide development. It zoned all the private land in the Park: parts can have very few buildings and other parts can have many. The APA tried to steer development to the villages and leave the open space as it was. It tried to make sure that buildings fit into the Adirondack environment.

The state-owned land was zoned, too. The Forest Preserve is now divided into *Wild Forest*, *Primitive* and *Wilderness* areas. Half the state land is zoned Wilderness — about a million acres. That is half the protected wilderness in the eastern United States.

Designated Wilderness areas can have no permanent structures except state-built lean-tos. Even most of the fire towers have been torn down. No motorized vehicles are allowed in these areas. Trails can be maintained, but chainsaws are banned except for a few weeks in the spring.

In the rest of the Forest Preserve, "Forever Wild" really means forever almost wild. Some roads are allowed, and snowmobile trails have been marked. Snowmobilers and fishermen with float planes have access to some of the preserve, while the zoning keeps the heart of the wilderness safe.

The commission's plan tried to balance development and preservation. Many preservationists now say that it allowed too much development, but in 1971, and for many years after, most Adirondack residents fought the APA in every way they could. The Adirondacks have always been a poor area. Jobs are scarce and precious. Adirondackers argued that APA rules kept development out of the mountains, and that without development there would be no jobs.

In fact, the very idea of an APA bothered them. Adirondack-

*Is this the way Adirondack waterfront should be developed?*
*(Photo © Alan Cederstrom; courtesy the Adirondack Council)*

ers did not want a government agency telling them what they could do with their land. They believed that the APA was tearing their last bit of independence away from them. There were lawsuits and angry meetings. One night in 1975 someone dumped a truck load of manure on the front yard of the APA headquarters. Robert Glennon, the APA's counsel, was assaulted. Most Adirondack opposition was peaceful, of course. But few Park residents supported the agency.

The APA's supporters replied that development would ruin the Adirondacks. "Forever Wild" and the open private lands made the Park unique, they said, and that uniqueness was needed to protect Adirondack jobs. Too many resorts and drive-ins and "tourist traps" would make the region look like anywhere else. The tourists would stop coming. Letting development run uncontrolled, they argued, was like killing the goose that laid the golden egg.

The supporters of the APA agreed that it limited Adirondackers' independence. But they pointed out that this had never been a real independence. Adirondack residents have never controlled their history. The mines, the logging camps and the hotels were all there because people outside the mountains wanted Adirondack iron, wood or fresh air.

Many Adirondackers still resent the APA, but some have come to agree with the ideas behind it. They value the open spaces of the Park as much as anyone else, and they agree that the state must keep the Park special. They know, too, that big development — summer or weekend homes for outsiders — creates few permanent jobs and many problems. And they realize that living in a special place gives them special responsibilities, even if they dislike outsiders telling them that.

The state Department of Environmental Conservation (DEC) has changed, too. It is now much more open to the value of wilderness, and it is trying to rebuild the ecosystem. The falcon, the eagle and the lynx have been brought back. Wandering male moose have begun to appear in the mountains, and the DEC is bringing in females. Some of nature's balance is being restored.

This is good news, but not all the news is good. The APA cannot end all of the Adirondacks' problems. One unsolved problem is acid precipitation. Coal-burning power plants, cars and factories pour chemicals into the air. These chemicals combine with water vapor and become acid. Acid rain or snow, sometimes as strong as vinegar, falls on the mountains, often hundreds of miles from the smokestacks that cause it. Because Adirondack soil is so thin and the rock underneath so hard, nothing neutralizes the acid. Many lakes have become so acidic that no fish can live there, and fish-eating birds like loons have vanished from them.

*Adirondack residents have lost many year-round jobs. This is the flooded pit of the Benson Mine in Star Lake, once the largest open-pit magnetite (iron ore) mine in the world, and the object in the center is the top of a smokestack. Eight hundred people used to work here. After the mine closed the weight of the water that filled it caused small earthquakes. (Photo by author)*

Even more frightening is "spruce die-off." The High Peaks below timberline are covered with spruce forest. Today half those spruce are dead, and acid rain is partly to blame. From the High Peaks today you see many patches of dry, brownish-grey forest.

New York cannot stop acid rain by itself. Most of the problem begins in other states. New York has joined with other northeastern states and with Canada to try to get federal laws that will reduce acid rain. This has been a slow and hard business. It will cost governments, industry and consumers a lot of money to stop acid precipitation. A new Clean Air Act has finally been

*These bears feasting at the Town of Webb dump have come to depend on garbage for their food. They are not tame, but they can hardly be called "wild" any more. (Photo by author)*

passed, but it is not as strong as environmentalists would like. It will take many years to see if it is strong enough.

Another problem is over-hiking. There are many quiet places in the Park, but on clear fall weekends over 150 climbers a day hike up Mount Marcy. Popular trails have become pools of mud and tangles of roots. Fragile alpine plants have been trampled. Thoughtless hikers have left tons of garbage at campsites.

The DEC and groups like the Adirondack Mountain Club have rebuilt trails. They have tried to steer hikers to areas that may be less popular but are often just as beautiful. The state has torn down some lean-tos and banned camping at high altitudes. These changes have helped, although on long weekends the main trails in the High Peaks can still seem like busy city streets.

Outside the Forest Preserve land there are other problems. Development has not gone away. Lumbering has become less profitable, so land speculators have bought up lumber company land to divide and sell for a fast profit. Advertisements invite city dwellers to "own your own piece of wilderness."

The APA cannot stop this. Under its rules half a million more houses could be built inside the Park. Lakeshores are especially threatened. Many lakes that were wild in 1971 are now ringed with vacation homes.

The war over development has heated up once more. In 1989 New York's Governor Mario Cuomo appointed a Commission on the Adirondacks in the Twenty-first Century. The commission recommended more controls on development. Buildings should be kept away from lakeshores, it said, and large properties should be kept open.

The commission urged the state to add about 655,000 acres to the Forest Preserve, to bring the state land to 3,100,000 acres — about 52 percent of the Park. The rest of the Park, it said, should be villages or productive forest land. Tax help for the lumber companies and aid to local communities would ensure both open space and a stable economy for Adirondack residents.

The commission paid close attention to the needs of the Park's residents. Many Adirondackers, though, took a quick look at the new development controls and rejected the whole report — even the parts urging roads, jobs and medical clinics. Instead of finding a compromise between development and preservation, the commissioners found themselves in the middle of another battle.

The commission's compromise seems the best way to preserve an Adirondack Park with room for both people and wilderness. Many of its ideas may still become law, although this will take a lot of work and some good fortune.

The Adirondacks have been fortunate before, though. There were no great riches under the mountains, so large-scale mining was worthwhile in only a few towns. The ruined hillsides and abandoned coal mines of another American mountain range, the Appalachians of Kentucky and West Virginia, show what could have happened to the Adirondacks.

The Adirondacks were fortunate, too, that "Forever Wild" became law, and that people learned over the years what "Forever Wild" could mean. They were fortunate to have people who came to know and love them, who hiked and canoed the forests and lakes, wrote about them, and fought to protect them.

We can hope that the Adirondacks will have more good fortune, that wilderness and villages will both be preserved, and that the people who read the speculators' ads will see how false they are. Nobody can "own" a piece of the wilderness. That, if anything, is the meaning of "Forever Wild" and the greatest lesson the Adirondacks can teach us.

For thousands of years we have tried to rule over nature. We have judged it by our own needs and tastes, turned forests into farms and cities and parks, and somehow we have not been satisfied. As we asked more and more of nature it seemed to give us less and less.

In a few special places, though, we have turned away from our selfishness. In the Adirondack Park we made a decision. In the public lands we would ask nothing of nature. Trees would grow and age and fall, rocks would break in the spring melt, animals would thrive or die. We gave up our claim to rule over nature.

That refusal to rule opened up the Adirondack wilderness to us. Because we asked nothing of nature, nature gave us everything: the great forests, the thousands of lakes and the uncounted waterfalls, each one different; the rocky peaks with the flowers that bloom for a week in the everlasting wind. The mountains falling away forever, the sun-warmed ledges of rock by the icy streams, the grey light of October mornings, the mist rising everywhere as the birds wake and call — all these are ours, so long as we do not try to claim them for ourselves.

For a billion years the Adirondack region has been a special place, with its own rocks, forests and animals. And a hundred years of "Forever Wild" has made it more special and more valuable than ever. Its villages and history are as fascinating as its beauty, for a hundred thousand people have lived and worked next to wilderness forests without destroying them: turn away from any Adirondack village, walk a mile or two from the road, and you will see a world in which people are still strangers. In a world of cities and factories, the Adirondacks have been set aside, thanks to our decision to turn so much of them back to nature. So long as we keep our side of that bargain, the Adirondacks will remain our wilderness.

## More Reading

THERE ARE FEW BOOKS about the Adirondacks written specifically for young readers. Of those intended for adults, the following are essential for any Adirondack library:

The best introduction to the area remains William Chapman White's *Adirondack Country*. White was a New York newspaperman who spent as much time as he could in the mountains. His book is both a history and an evocation of the area. He died in 1955, a year after it was published. His widow has added chapters bringing his story up to 1971 and the APA, but White's writing doesn't date at all.

The best general history is *The Adirondack Park: A Political History* by Frank Graham. Graham is not a New Yorker; he places "Forever Wild" in a national context, and his book is richer for it.

Any collection of Adirondack books should include *The Adirondack Reader*, edited by Paul Jamieson, Professor Emeritus of English at St. Lawrence University, northwest of the Park. The *Reader* collects nearly 400 years of writing about the Adirondacks. Not the least of its charms is Jamieson's own commentary.

Several excellent collections of photographs are available. None captures the special character of the area's light and landscape better than Nathan Farb's two books, *The Adirondacks* and *100 Adirondack Views*.

There are many books about the natural history of the Park. A good starting point is the *Adirondack Wildguide* by Michael G. DiNunzio.

Stories, essays, photographs, and current news and commentary can be found in the fine bimonthly *Adirondack Life*.

# INDEX

(Italics refer to illustrations)

[ 99 ]

## About the author

Michael Steinberg lives a little too far away from the Adirondacks with his wife, their son, a dog and two cats. He works as a lawyer, keeps house, and in his spare time tries to figure out how everything got the way it is. This is his first book.